CRISTAL COOPER

NEW BEGINNING

The Essential Guide on How to Transform to a New and Better You, Discover Self-Improvement Tips and How to Believe in Yourself To Get a New and Better You

Descrierea CIP a Bibliotecii Naționale a României
CRISTAL COOPER
   NEW BEGINNING. The Essential Guide on How to
Transform to a New and Better You, Discover Self-Improvement
Tips and How to Believe in Yourself To Get a New and Better
You / Cristal Cooper – Bucharest: Editura My Ebook, 2021
   ISBN

CRISTAL COOPER

NEW BEGINNING

The Essential Guide on How to Transform to a New and Better You, Discover Self-Improvement Tips and How to Believe in Yourself To Get a New and Better You

My Ebook Publishing House
Bucharest, 2021

CRISTAL COOPER

NEW BEGINNING

The Essential Guide on How to Transform to a New and Better You, Discover Self-improvement Tips and Tricks to Believe in Yourself To Get a New and Better You

MW Book Publishing House
Bucharest 2021

Believing In Yourself And Your Abilities Is Absolutely The Most Important Thing You Can Do On Your Journey To A New Better You.

It is critical to develop the self-confidence you need to carry you through to the realization of your goals.

Self-confidence is a bit different from self-esteem. Self-esteem refers to your feelings about yourself, your behaviors and your worth as a person. Self-confidence is your belief in your abilities and in the way you present yourself to the world. The actions of others are more likely to erode your self-confidence rather than your self-esteem. However, the two emotions have quite a bit in common. Both are measures of your inherent or developed belief in yourself- and both can be easily pushed off balance, resulting in either over-confident or defeatist behaviors that distance you from your ultimate objectives.

You need to create a balance between too little self-confidence and too much. You cannot accomplish anything without self-confidence; on the other hand, too much self-confidence can ensure that you don't try hard enough to reach your goals, and you will fall short of realizing your possibilities.

Once you understand that you truly can do anything you put your mind to, you will have unlocked the key to positive thinking. There is no limit to the power of the human mind. Your possibilities really are endless.

You can help yourself build self-confidence through a simple daily exercise you develop yourself after learning the basic premise. Like most of the practices for working with self-improvement, you may feel ridiculous at first. Here are the basic steps to your daily self-confidence routine, which is best performed in the morning as you prepare to face the day:

- **Decimate distractions.** You need this time to yourself. You *deserve* this time to yourself. While you're performing your self-confidence routine, don't answer the phone, check your e-mail, watch television, or listen to the radio. Let household members know that this time is your time, and you would prefer not to be disturbed.

- **Get physical.** Pamper yourself with your daily physical preparations. When you shower, use your favorite soap or scented body wash. Choose clothing that makes you feel good and matches your mood. Make yourself comfortable with the way you look, and your self-confidence will rise to match it.

- **Focus forward.** As you get ready, reflect on what you want to accomplish for the day. Be sure to consider the mood you want to set for yourself as well as any goals or objectives you will reach. You might even partake in a quick receptive visualization session to see yourself reaching your goals and cement them in your mind.

- **Get pumped.** Now comes the ridiculous part. Stand in front of a mirror, look yourself in the eyes, and sing your own praises. Out loud. Tell yourself that you are the person you want to be; that you possess worthwhile qualities; that you can do that which you are now setting out to do. Be as specific as possible. Instead of saying, "I am competent," say: "I know how to handle problems when they arise." The more specific you are, the more effective your self-confidence routine will prove to be.

Self-confidence is the glue that holds your personality together. If you are serious about changing your life, developing a healthy self-confidence will equip you to do it quickly and effortlessly. Don't let fear, worry and doubt keep you from blossoming into confidence. You can accomplish anything, as long as you believe you can. It really is as simple as that.

Self-improvement & Success – Hand in Hand

Ask any business owner and you'll find out that rewards are one of the most powerful motivators. People are more willing to work toward a goal when they know they will get something out of it at the end. Since your boss probably won't reward you for losing weight or remodeling your bathroom, you can plan to give yourself a reward when you meet a given goal.

When selecting self-rewards, be sure to match them to your goals. This will not only ensure you don't get tired of the same reward, but will also help you when you're planning the strategies you'll use to accomplish your aims. For example, if you'd like to spend less time watching television and more time outside or with your family, you can reward yourself with a trip to the theater to see a great movie. If you're planning to quit smoking, part of your strategy could be to set aside some of the money you'll save by not buying cigarettes and get yourself a new outfit, or something you've had your eye on for a while but haven't been able to afford.

Some goals come with intrinsic rewards already built in, yours for the claiming when you reach your objective. For example, if you're going to start your own business, you already know you'll be rewarded by working for yourself, possibly even by working out of your home. Whether you're working for an intrinsic reward or providing yourself with an incentive, treating yourself is a great way to generate enthusiasm for the task at hand.

Everything that happens to us happens in purpose. And sometimes, one thing leads to another. Instead of locking yourself up in your cage of fears and crying over past heartaches, embarrassment and failures, treat them as your teachers and they will become your tools in both self-improvement and success.

Remember watching Patch Adams? It's one great film that will help you improve yourself. Hunter "patch" Adams is a medical student who failed to make it through the board exams. After months of suffering in melancholy, depression and suicidal attempts – he decided to seek for medical attention and voluntarily admitted himself in a psychiatric ward. His months of stay in the hospital led him to meeting different kinds of people.

Sick people in that matter. He met a catatonic, a mentally retarded, a schizophrenic and so on. Patch found ways of treating his own ailment and finally realized he has to get back on track. He woke up one morning realizing that after all the failure and pains he has gone through, he still want to become a doctor. He carries with himself a positive attitude that brought him self-improvement and success. He didn't only improved himself, but also the life of the people around him and the quality of life. Did he succeed? Needless to say, he became the best damn doctor his country has ever known.

So, when does self-improvement become synonymous with success? Where do we start? Take these tips:

- **Stop thinking and feeling as if you're a failure, <u>because you're not</u>**. How can others accept you if YOU can't accept YOU?

- **When you see hunks and models on TV, think more on self-improvement, not self pitying**. Self-acceptance is not just about having nice slender legs, or great abs. Concentrate on inner beauty.

- **When people feel so down and low about themselves, help them move up**. Don't go down with them. They'll pull you down further and both of you will end up feeling inferior.

- **The world is a large room for lessons, not mistakes**. Don't feel stupid and doomed forever just because you failed on a science quiz. There's always a next time. Make rooms for self-improvement.

- **Take things one at a time**. You don't expect black sheep's to be goody-two-shoes in just a snap of a finger. Self-improvement is a one day at a time process.

- **Self-improvement results to inner stability, personality development and SUCCESS**. It comes from self-confidence, self-appreciation and self-esteem.

- **Set meaningful and achievable goals**. Self-improvement doesn't turn you to be the exact replica of Cameron Diaz or Ralph Fiennes. It hopes and aims to result to an improved and better YOU.

- **Little things mean BIG to other people**. Sometimes, we don't realize that the little things that we do like a pat on the back, saying "hi" or "hello", greeting someone "good day" or telling Mr. Smith something like "hey, I love your tie!" are simple things that mean so much to other people. When we're being appreciative about beautiful things around us and other people, we also become beautiful to them.

- **When you're willing to accept change and go through the process of self-improvement, it doesn't mean that everyone else is**. The world is a place where people of different values and attitude hang out. Sometimes, even if you think you and your best friend always like to do the same thing together at the same time, she would most likely decline an invitation for self-improvement.

We should always remember that there's no such thing as 'overnight success'. It's always a wonderful feeling to hold on to the things that you already have now, realizing that those are just one of the things you once wished for. A very nice quote says that, *"When the student is ready, the teacher will appear."* We are all here to learn our lessons. Our parents, school teachers, friends, colleagues, officemates, neighbors… they are our teachers. When we open our doors for self-improvement, we increase our chances to head to the road of success.

The Importance of Improving Yourself

Sometimes, when all our doubts, fears and insecurities wrap ourselves up, we always come up with the idea of "*I wish I was somebody else.*" More often than not, we think and believe that someone or rather, most people are better than us - when in reality, the fact is, **most people are more scared than us**.

You spot a totally eye-catching girl sitting by herself at a party, casually sipping on a glass of Asti Spumanti. You think to yourself, "she looks so perfectly calm and confident." But if you could read thru her transparent mind, you would see a bunch of clouds of thoughts and you might just be amazed that she's thinking "are people talking about why I am seated here alone?... Why don't guys find me attractive? ...I don't like my ankles, they look too skinny... I wish I was as intelligent as my best friend."

We look at a young business entrepreneur and say "*Wooh... what else could he ask for?*" He stares at himself at the mirror and murmur to himself, "I hate my big eyes... I wonder why my friends won't talk to me... I hope mom and dad would still work things out."

Isn't it funny? We look at other people, envy them for looking so outrageously perfect and wish we could trade places with them, while they look at us and thinks of the same thing. We are insecure of other people who themselves are insecure of us. We suffer from low self-esteem, lack of self-confidence and lose hope in self-improvement because we are enveloped in quiet desperation.

Sometimes, you notice that you have an irritating habit like biting off your finger nails, having a foul mouth, and you – of all people, is the last to know.

I have a friend who never gets tired of talking. And in most conversations, she is the only one who seems to be interested in the things she has to say. So all of our other friends tend to avoid the circles whenever she's around, and she doesn't notices how badly she became socially handicapped – gradually affecting the people in her environment.

One key to self-improvement is to LISTEN and TALK to a trusted friend. Find someone who you find comfort in opening up with even the most gentle topics you want to discuss. Ask questions like "do you think I am ill-mannered?", "Do I always sound so argumentative?", "Do I talk too loud?", "Does my breath smell?", "Do I ever bore you when were together?". In this way, the other person will obviously know that you are interested in the process of self-improvement. Lend her your ears for comments and criticisms and don't give her answers like "Don't exaggerate! That's just the way I am!" Open up your mind and heart as well. And in return, you may want to help your friend with constructive criticism that will also help her improve herself.

One of Whitney Houston's songs says *"Learning to love yourself is the greatest love of all."* **True enough**! In order to love others, you must love yourself too. Remember, you cannot give what you do not have.

Before telling other people some ways on how to improve themselves, let them see that you yourself is a representation and a product of self-improvement. Self-improvement makes us better people, we then inspire other people, and then the rest of the world will follow.

Stop thinking of yourselves as second-rate beings. Forget the repetitive thought of "If only I was richer... if only I was thinner" and so on. Accepting your true self is the first step to self-improvement. We need to stop comparing ourselves to others only to find out at the end that we've got 10 more reasons to envy them.

We all have our insecurities. Nobody is perfect. We always wish we had better things, better features, better body parts, etc.

But life need not to be perfect for people to be happy about themselves.

Self-improvement and loving yourself is not a matter of shouting to the whole world that you are perfect and you are the best. It's the virtue of acceptance and contentment. When we begin to improve ourselves, we then begin to feel contented and happy.

Building Your Self-Esteem

So how do you stay calm, composed and maintain self-esteem in a tough environment? Here are some tips you may to consider as a starter guide to self-improvement.

Imagine yourself as a Dart Board. Everything and everyone else around you may become Dart Pins, at one point or another. These dart pins will destroy your self-esteem and pull you down in ways you won't even remember. Don't let them destroy you, or get the best of you. So which dart pins should you avoid?

Dart Pin #1 : Negative Work Environment

Beware of "dog eat dog" theory where everyone else is fighting just to get ahead. This is where non-appreciative people usually thrive. No one will appreciate your contributions even if you miss lunch and dinner, and stay up late. Most of the time you get to work too much without getting help from people concerned. Stay out of this, it will ruin your self-esteem. Competition is at stake anywhere. Be healthy enough to compete, but in a healthy competition that is.

Dart Pin #2: Other People's Behavior

Bulldozers, brown nosers, gossipmongers, whiners, backstabbers, snipers, people walking wounded, controllers, naggers, complainers, exploders, patronizers, sluffers… all these kinds of people will pose bad vibes for your self-esteem, as well as to your self-improvement scheme.

Dart Pin #3: Changing Environment

You can't be a green bug on a brown field. Changes challenge our paradigms. It tests our flexibility, adaptability and alters the way we think. Changes will make life difficult for awhile, it may cause stress but it will help us find ways to improve our selves. Change will be there forever, we must be susceptible to it.

Dart Pin #4: Past Experience

It's okay to cry and say "ouch!" when we experience pain. But don't let pain transform itself into fear. It might grab you by the tail and swing you around. Treat each failure and mistake as a lesson.

Dart Pin #5: Negative World View

Look at what you're looking at. Don't wrap yourself up with all the negativities of the world. In building self-esteem, we must learn how to make the best out of worst situations.

Dart Pin #6: Determination Theory

The way you are and your behavioral traits is said to be a mixed end product of your inherited traits (genetics), your upbringing (psychic), and your environmental surroundings such as your spouse, the company, the economy or your circle of friends. You have your own identity. If your father is a failure, it doesn't mean you have to be a failure too. Learn from other people's experience, so you'll never have to encounter the same mistakes.

Sometimes, you may want to wonder if some people are born leaders or positive thinkers. NO. **Being positive, and staying positive is a choice**. Building self-esteem and drawing lines for self-improvement is a choice, not a rule or a talent. God wouldn't come down from heaven and tell you – "George, you may now have the permission to build self-esteem and improve yourself."

In life, it's hard to stay tough especially when things and people around you keep pulling you down. When we get to the battlefield, we should choose the right luggage to bring and armors to use, and pick those that are bullet proof. Life's options give us arrays of more options. Along the battle, we will get hit and bruised. And wearing a bulletproof armor ideally means 'self-change'. The kind of change which comes from within. Voluntarily. Armor or Self Change changes 3 things: our attitude, our behavior and our way of thinking.

Building self-esteem will eventually lead to self-improvement if we start to become responsible for who we are, what we have and what we do. Its like a flame that should gradually spread like a brush fire from inside and out. When we develop self-esteem, we take control of our mission, values and discipline. Self-esteem brings about self-improvement, true assessment, and determination. So how do you start putting up the building blocks of self-esteem? Be positive. Be contented and happy. Be appreciative. Never miss an opportunity to compliment. A positive way of living will help you build self-esteem, your starter guide to self-improvement.

Motivation: The Heart of Self-Improvement

Pain may sometimes be the reason why people change. Getting flunked grades make us realize that we need to study. Debts remind us of our inability to look for a source of income. Being humiliated gives us the 'push' to speak up and fight for ourselves to save our face from the next embarrassments. It may be a bitter experience, a friend's tragic story, a great movie, or an inspiring book that will help us get up and get just the right amount of motivation we need in order to improve ourselves.

With the countless negativities the world brings about, how do we keep motivated? Try on the tips I prepared from **A to Z**!

Achieve your dreams. Avoid negative people, things and places. Eleanor Roosevelt once said, "the future belongs to those who believe in the beauty of their dreams."

Believe in yourself, and in what you can do.

Consider things on every angle and aspect. Motivation comes from determination. To be able to understand life, you should feel the sun from both sides.

Don't give in and don't give up. Thomas Edison failed once, twice, more than thrice before he came up with his invention and perfected the incandescent light bulb. Make motivation as your steering wheel.

Enjoy. Work as if you don't need money. Dance as if nobody's watching. Love as if you never cried. Learn as if you'll live forever. Motivation takes place when people are happy.

Family and Friends – are life's greatest 'F' treasures. Don't lose sight of them.

Give more than what is enough. Where does motivation and self-improvement take place at work? At home? At school? When you exert extra effort in doing things.

Hang on to your dreams. They may dangle in there for a moment, but these little stars will be your driving force.

Ignore those who try to destroy you. Don't let other people to get the best of you. Stay out of toxic people – the kind of friends who hates to hear about your success.

Just be yourself. The key to success is to be yourself. And the key to failure is to try to please everyone.

Keep trying no matter how hard life may seem. When a person is motivated, eventually he sees a harsh life finally clearing out, paving the way to self-improvement.

Learn to love yourself. Now isn't that easy?

Make things happen. Motivation is when your dreams are put into work clothes.

Never lie, cheat or steal. Always play a fair game.

Open your eyes. People should learn the horse attitude and horse sense. They see things in 2 ways – how they want things to be, and how they should be.

Practice makes perfect. Practice is about motivation. It lets us learn repertoire and ways on how can we recover from our mistakes.

Quitters never win. And winners never quit. So, choose your fate – are you going to be a quitter? Or a winner?

Ready yourself. Motivation is also about preparation. We must hear the little voice within us telling us to get started before others will get on their feet and try to push us around. Remember, it wasn't raining when Noah build the ark.

Stop procrastinating!

Take control of your life. Discipline or self-control jives synonymously with motivation. Both are key factors in self-improvement.

Understand others. If you know very well how to talk, you should also learn how to listen. Yearn to understand first, and to be understood the second.

Visualize it. Motivation without vision is like a boat on a dry land.

Want it more than anything. Dreaming means believing. And to believe is something that is rooted out from the roots of motivation and self-improvement.

X Factor is what will make you different from the others. When you are motivated, you tend to put on "extras" on your life like extra time for family, extra help at work, extra care for friends, and so on.

You are unique. No one in this world looks, acts, or talks like you. Value your life and existence, because you're just going to spend it once.

Zero in on your dreams and go for it!!!

Unlocking Your Self Improvement Power

When we look at a certain object, a painting for example – we won't be able to appreciate what's in it, what is painted and what else goes with it if the painting is just an inch away from our face. But if we try to take it a little further, we'll have a clearer vision of the whole artwork.

We reach a point in our life when we are ready for change and a whole bunch of information that will help us unlock our self-improvement power. Until then, something can be staring us right under our nose but we don't see it. The only time we think of unlocking our self-improvement power is when everything got worst.

24

Take the frog principle for example.

Try placing Frog A in a pot of boiling water. What happens? He twerps! He jumps off! Why? Because he is not able to tolerate sudden change in his environment – the water's temperature. Then try Frog B: place him in a lukewarm water, then turn the gas stove on. Wait until the water reaches a certain boiling point. Frog B then thinks "Ooh… it's a bit warm in here".

People are like Frog B in general. Today, Anna thinks Carl hates her. Tomorrow, Patrick walks up to her and told her he hates her. Anna stays the same and doesn't mind her what her friends says. The next day, she learned that Kim and John also abhors her. Anna doesn't realize at once the importance and the need for self-improvement until the entire community hates her.

We learn our lessons when we experience pain. We finally see the warning signs and signals when things get rough and tough. When do we realize that we need to change diets? When none of our jeans and shirts would fit us. When do we stop eating candies and chocolates? When all of our teeth has fallen off. When do we realize that we need to stop smoking? When our lungs have gone bad. When do we pray and ask for help? When we realize that we're gonna die tomorrow.

The only time most of us ever learn about unlocking our self-improvement power is when the whole world is crashing and falling apart. We think and feel this way because it is not easy to change. But change becomes more painful when we ignore it.

Change will happen, like it or hate it. At one point or another, we are all going to experience different turning points in our life – and we are all going to eventually unlock our self-improvement power not because the world says so, not because our friends are nagging us, but because we realized its for our own good.

Happy people don't just accept change, they embrace it. Now, you don't have to feel a tremendous heat before realizing the need for self-improvement. Unlocking your self-improvement power means unlocking yourself up in the cage of thought that "its just the way I am". It is such a poor excuse for people who fear and resist change. Most of us program our minds like computers.

Jen repeatedly tells everyone that she doesn't have the guts to be around groups of people. She heard her mom, her dad, her sister, her teacher tell the same things about her to other people. Over the years, that is what Jen believes. She believes its her story. And what happens? Every time a great crowd would troop over their house, in school, and in the community – she tends to step back, shy away and lock herself up in a room. Jen didn't only believed in her story, she lived it.

Jen has to realize that she is not what she is in her story. Instead of having her story post around her face for everyone to remember, she has to have the spirit and show people "I am an important person and I should be treated accordingly!"

Self-improvement may not be everybody's favorite word, but if we look at things in a different point of view, we might have greater chances of enjoying the whole process instead of counting the days until we are fully improved. Three sessions in a week at the gym would result to a healthier life, reading books instead of watching TV will shape up a more profound knowledge, going out with friends and peers will help you take a step back from work and unwind. And just when you are enjoying the whole process of unlocking your self-improvement power, you'll realize that you're beginning to take things light and become happy.

Now for the…

Crash Course 7-Day Program to Self-Improvement

I seem to lost count on how many times I've read and heard of celebrity marriages failing almost left and right. Not that I care (and personally I don't), it seems strange that we often see movie and TV stars as flawless people, living the fairytale life of riches and glamour. I suppose we all have to stop sticking our heads in the clouds and face reality.

There are many ways to lose your sense of self-esteem despite of how trivial it could get. But whatever happens, we should all try not to lose our own sense of self.

So what does it take to be a cut above the rest? Here are some of the things you can think and improve on that should be enough for a week.

Day 1: Know your purpose.

Are you wandering through life with little direction - hoping that you'll find happiness, health and prosperity? Identify your life purpose or mission statement and you will have your own unique compass that will lead you to your truth north every time.

This may seem tricky at first when you see yourself to be in a tight or even dead end. But there's always that little loophole to turn things around and you can make a big difference to yourself.

Day 2: Know your values.

What do you value most? Make a list of your top 5 values. Some examples are security, freedom, family, spiritual development, learning. As you set your goals for 2005 - check your goals against your values. If the goal doesn't align with any of your top five values - you may want to reconsider it or revise it.

The number shouldn't discourage you, instead it should motivate you to do more than you can ever dreamed of.

Day 3: Know your needs.

Unmet needs can keep you from living authentically. Take care of yourself. Do you have a need to be acknowledged, to be right, to be in control, to be loved? There are so many people who lived their lives without realizing their dreams and most of them end up being stressed or even depressed for that matter. List your top four needs and get them met before it's too late!

Day 4: Know your passions.

You know who you are and what you truly enjoy in life. Obstacles like doubt and lack of enthusiasm will only hinder you, but will not derail your chance to become the person you ought to be. Express yourself and honor the people who has inspired you to become the very person you wanted to be.

Day 5: Live from the inside out.

Increase your awareness of your inner wisdom by regularly reflecting in silence. Commune with nature. Breathe deeply to quiet your distracted mind. For most of us city slickers it's hard to even find the peace and quiet we want even in our own home. In my case I often just sit in a dimly lit room and play some classical music. There's sound, yes, but music does soothe the savage beast.

Day 6: Honor your strengths.

What are your positive traits? What special talents do you have? List three - if you get stuck, ask those closest to you to help identify these. Are you imaginative, witty, good with your hands? Find ways to express your authentic self through your strengths. You can increase your self-confidence when you can share what you know to others.

Day 7: Serve others.

When you live authentically, you may find that you develop an interconnected sense of being. When you are true to who you are, living your purpose and giving of your talents to the world around you, you give back in service what you came to share with others -your spirit - your essence. The rewards for sharing your gift with those close to you is indeed rewarding, much more if it were to be the eyes of a stranger who can appreciate what you have done to them.

Self-improvement is indeed one type of work that is worth it. It shouldn't always be within the confines of an office building, or maybe in the four corners of your own room. The difference lies within ourselves and how much we want to change for the better.

Exercises that reinforce positive thinking

In order to reap the personal and professional benefits of positive thinking, you must first train your mind to think positively automatically – without you consciously having to decide to "be positive". To do this you will need to take certain steps. First, you will need to make a conscious decision to pursue positive thinking and then commit wholeheartedly to realizing that goal. In order for positive thinking to have an impact on your life you will also need to believe in its benefits. And, since there will be setbacks throughout your journey, you will need the power of your convictions to help keep you on track.

Once you have committed to learning the skills of positive thinking, you will need to use certain exercises to teach yourself the methods and to reinforce the affirmative thoughts in your mind. The following is a list of ways to learn and practice the art of positive thinking.

Review your self-talk- The first step to learning positive thinking skills is to review the type of thinking you are currently engaging in now. Think back to the last bad day that you had.

How did you react? What types of things were you saying to yourself, both internally and out loud? What feelings did you have immediately about the situation? What feelings did you take away from the situation? How do you feel about the situation now?

The answers to the above questions will give you a pretty good idea of what type of self-talk you usually engage in. For example, did you beat yourself up about the problem? Did your mind search for ways in which the problem was ultimately your fault? Did you blame the incident on bad luck?

In order to visualize the difference between positive self-talk and negative self-talk, let's compare the two habits using the same situation. For this example, let's assume that Sally, a stay-at-home seamstress, started an internet business to sell her handmade handbags. Once the business began to grow, she hired another woman to sew some of the bags for her. Recently, ten of these bags were returned due to defects.

Example #1- negative self-talk: In this example, you will read some things that Sally said or thought to herself upon receiving the returned handbags.

> "I should have looked the bags over more carefully, I knew I would mess this up."

"Why did I think I would ever be able to succeed in this business?"

"This is the end, now no one will want to buy these bags."

"Everyone said I couldn't make it and they were right."

"I am such an idiot, how could I make a mistake like this."

"If it wasn't for bad luck I wouldn't have any luck at all."

"Why I am so stupid?"

Example #2-positive self-talk: Here, you will read some affirmative things that Sally thought or said out loud to herself.

"Well, of course, this is a setback, but it will give me the opportunity to sharpen my customer service skills."

"While I did forget to pay attention to the details for a moment, I have learned a valuable lesson."

"Luckily, it was only ten bags and the problem was caught before it was serious."

"Every business has its pitfalls. I am going to use this one to help me do better next time."

As you can see from the examples, how we choose to see a situation can make all the difference in its outcome. When our mind talks, our attitude listens and responds. Because of this correlation, we have the power to literally "talk" ourselves into or out of success and satisfaction.

When we engage in negative self-talk we convince ourselves that our efforts are futile. This belief leads to feelings of worthlessness and failure. These feelings make it easier for us to fall victim to even more negative thoughts, which eventually snowball into feelings of despair and defeat.

However, when we engage in positive self-talk, we convince our minds and ourselves that all things are possible. By focusing on the positive we are able to believe in and realize a desirable outcome. If you truly believe that you can turn a negative situation into a positive asset then you will. Through repeated positive self-talk you will see any possible affirmative outcome as a fact of life not as an impossible dream.

To begin changing our self-talk from the negative to the positive, we must first look to the truth of the situation. When you find yourself faced with a problem, begin your thought process with a review of the facts. This initial review should not include any feelings or predictions. To help with this process, ask yourself the following questions.

1. What was the actual, physical cause of this problem? In Sally's case, the *physical* cause of the problem was not

35

her lack of attention to detail; rather, it was a mistake in the construction of the handbag.

2. What factual events lead up to the problem? Again, using Sally's case, the actual event could have been miscommunication in the sewing instructions, a misunderstanding of the process on the part of her employee or an oversight by her employee. In any case, the event was unintentional and in no way a reflection of Sally's overall performance or business success.

3. How bad is the situation, really? While a situation may seem overwhelming at first, rational thought usually leads to the realization that the problem is not as bad as it seems. Use this question to help you brainstorm some possible outcomes, both good and bad, which could realistically stem from the problem. In Sally's case, her first thought was that everyone would stop purchasing her handbags. Rationally, however, Sally could focus on the number of currently satisfied customers, the small number of unsatisfied customers and the knowledge that she still had the opportunity to make the situation right and win over the upset customers with exceptional customer service.

Once you have determined the facts of the situation, you need to review your feelings about the situation and determine the root of those feelings. To help sort your feelings out, ask yourself the following questions.

1. What part of the situation has upset you the most? Many times, the actual problem is not the source of a person's negative feelings; instead it is how the problem makes them feel about themselves. In Sally's case, the defect in the handbags wasn't the real problem. The real problem was that the defect caused Sally's biggest fear to seem substantiated. Upon deeper examination, Sally realized that the problem with the handbags brought out her feelings of insecurity. The moment that she was made aware of the problem she began to focus on her perceived lack of business skills.

2. Are your feelings based on the reality of the situation or on how you believe the situation to be? This is an important question to ask yourself, in that it will help you differentiate between fact and fiction. Is this problem truly a representation of who you are as a person and professional? Or, are you over dramatizing

the situation and placing unrealistic expectations on the subject at hand?

3. How have you handled feelings such as these in the past? In other words, are you truly reacting only to the present situation or are you falling back on old feelings and insecurities and letting these feelings cloud your judgment?

4. If this situation were happening to a colleague or friend of yours, how would you view the situation? Sometimes it helps to step away from a problem in order to view it more objectively.

Now that you have determined the reasons behind your self-talk habits, you can use that knowledge to shape new positive self-talk habits.

Practice positive self-talk- In order to turn your thinking around, you will need to consciously practice positive thinking. An excellent tool for this is the positive thinking game. In this game you will be required to state a positive outcome in response to a negative scenario. The following are a few examples to get you started. Each example contains a negative scenario and a possible positive response. Once you understand the technique, you will be able to create an endless supply of your own scenarios.

•The negative circumstance is that I lost the Wilbur account, however the positive circumstance is that I now have more time to devote to the Moore account.

•The negative circumstance is that my initial product is not selling very well, however the positive circumstance is that I can now devote my expertise to improving its original design.

•The negative circumstance is that sales in my field are at an all-time low, however the positive circumstance is that this period will give me the motivation I need to explore other, alternative markets for my product.

Make a list of the positives in your life- Once you are able to determine the positive in any given situation, you are ready to create a tangible reference list. Take a moment to jot down all of the positives in your life. Include such things as your health, your family, your previous education and training, any goals that you have realized, your personal and professional accomplishments, and the good points of your current business. List everything that you have to be thankful for or that you are happy about. List just as many small things as big things. You will want this list to be as complete as possible as you will be using it daily to keep your positive thinking training on track.

As the days and weeks go by, take the time to add new things to list as they happen or as they occur to you. Better yet, add to the list each night before you go to bed in order to end each day on a high note and prepare yourself to the start the next day in a positive state of mind.

Make a positive to-do list- Every morning, before you begin your day, make a positive to-do list that accentuates your goals for the day. For example, if you need to make a call to a client, do not simple write "call client" on your list. Instead, write the task in a positive manner, such as "call Mr. Williams and close the deal".

By writing out the task in an affirmative manner with a concrete positive outcome attached, your brain will be influenced to think of the task as completed and positive instead of as pending and open for failure.

You can also use the wording of each task to promote action. By being specific in your terms, you can turn a vague objective like "rework sales letter" into an action-orientated goal such as "rewrite the second paragraph of the sales letter to include two new benefits and change the deadline for membership to promote immediate ordering".

The goal of this type of to-do list is to positively influence your attitude and outlook for the day while strengthening your belief in desirable outcomes in order to keep motivation and focus high.

And, although it may seem silly, be sure to apply this same technique to your personal to-do list. Not only will this habit give you plenty of opportunities to practice your positive thinking skills, but it will also help you keep your energy and positive attitude up while you complete the necessary and sometimes mundane tasks of everyday life.

Take care of yourself both physically and mentally- In order to retain a positive outlook in life you need to feel good about yourself, both inside and out. In order to feel good about yourself you need to take care of yourself.

To meet this goal, it is usually easier to start with the physical aspects. If you don't already exercise daily, begin now. If you often skip breakfast, begin making it an integral part of your day. If you need a haircut, get one! Every step you take to improve your life or fix your self-perceived flaws will help build your self-confidence. Then, once your self-confidence is boosted, your positive thinking skills can flourish.

For internal change, begin by looking at your attitudes about yourself. Do you feel as though you need to learn more about a certain topic, such as internet marketing? If so, take a class or read a book about the topic. By increasing your knowledge you will decrease the severity of any insecurities that you may be harboring.

Do you have certain goals that you had planned to accomplish by this time in your life? The act of harboring unfinished business and unrealized dreams has a tendency to make us feel bad about ourselves. Start today with a small step toward your goal and commit to following through on the project. Just by beginning the process, you will immediately feel better about the situation and once you have attained the goal, your self-confidence will skyrocket.

Do you feel as though you never have enough time to accomplish your goals? Start by re-evaluating your time. First, delete time-wasting tasks from your daily schedule, and then carve out periods for finishing tasks. When rewriting your schedule, make sure to include time for relaxation and fun. Without downtime, your creative thoughts are unable to flourish.

42

The point of all of these exercises, both the positive thinking exercises and the self-improvement steps, is to put yourself in the correct frame of mind to accept a positive point of view. Through continued use of these exercises, you will eventually train your brain to think positively, automatically.

Use visualizations and affirmations to improve your positive thinking skills

Visualizations and affirmations are key tools in the quest for positive thinking skills. While the two exercises differ in technique, they both work to accomplish the same goal. Both exercises help to change your positive thinking goals from lofty dreams to achievable reality, however, visualizations work through imagery, while affirmations work through spoken statements.

Visualizations are key to the process of positive thinking because they offer you a way to "see" your goals as an actual outcome. This ability to see an outcome will give you control over that outcome. For instance, imagine that you are preparing to write the copy for your internet business's home page and you are not thinking positively about your writing skills. If you just use the facts about your product or service and transfer those facts to a written page, your copy could come out sounding flat and uninspired. However, by using visualization first, you will be able to prepare not just the facts but your attitude as well. Once you can visualize yourself writing the perfect, trust inspiring, buying motivated web copy, you will be able to write that copy.

The point of visualization is to use all of your senses to "see' yourself completing any task or solving any problem in a perfectly executed manner. By imagining an event in great detail and focusing on the desired outcome, you will program your mind and body to respond as if the visualized scenario was an expected event. By repeating this visualization frequently, you will train your mind to follow a pattern that leads to the desired outcome.

Thankfully, visualization is easy to learn. Take a moment to think about something that you are currently struggling with either in business or in your personal life. Now, concentrating on that situation, use the following steps to learn and practice the skill of visualization.

1. Clear your mind of all other thoughts and distractions. This step is important because it will enable you to fully concentrate on the image and allow you to follow the

imagery to the positive outcome without interruption. In the beginning, it will be easier to complete this step in a quiet environment where you can close your eyes, relax and be completely alone for several minutes.

2. Picture yourself completing the task or solving the problem in a positive way. Start at the beginning and actually envision yourself going through each step in the most positive, desirable way. Envision every detail about the situation in order to make the image seem more like fact than fantasy. Give attention to the clothes you are wearing, the people you are with, the actual words you are using and the words others are using in their responses to you.

3. Keep the outcome positive and perfect. The most important thing to remember when practicing visualization is that you must only picture the outcome in a positive way. Never picture yourself failing or even faltering. During visualization, always picture yourself performing in a perfect manner.

4. Once you have reached the end of the visualization, review it in your mind. Look for areas that you can improve upon during your next visualization session.

Add details where necessary and increase positive steps where you can.

5. Repeat the visualization often. While visualization can be a key step in positive thinking, it only works well when used frequently.

6. After you have accomplished the goal or solved the problem in real life, review the actual event and use visualization to change any negative circumstances into positive ones. If any detail of the actual event did not play out perfectly, envision that detail in a way that does. This step will help prime your mind to perform in a more desirable way the next time.

Now that you know how to practice visualization, it is time to learn more about affirmations. Affirmations are spoken statements that focus on the positive achievement of a goal. Affirmations differ from positive self-talk techniques in that they concentrate on more specific statements and are action-oriented. For example, if you are nervous about pitching a new idea to a customer your self-talk statement may be something like "I know this idea is a good one and my customer will be happy to hear about it." However, with an affirmation your statement would be more action driven, such as "Tomorrow morning I am pitching my new idea to Mr. Clark by pointing out the cost-saving benefits."

With positive self-talk you are attempting to bolster your positive attitude and belief in yourself. With affirmations you are stating a goal in a way that makes your subconscious believe that the event is already a fact. This subconscious belief is accomplished through three unique steps. First, affirmations are always spoken in first person narrative. This personalization of the fact allows the subconscious to more readily accept the statement. For example, instead of saying, "My customers are happy with my service", you would say "I know that my service/product makes my customers happy".

Second, affirmations are always stated in the present tense. By using words such as "I am" or "I know," you are tricking your mind into believing that the statement is already happening. Whereas, using statements such as "I will" or "I think" allows doubt to creep into your subconscious.

Third, affirmations are always positive in nature. For a statement to qualify as an affirmation it has to be worded without any negative language. For example, the statement "I am qualified to write excellent web copy" is an affirmation. The statement "I will try to write decent web copy" is not.

Now that you understand the nature of affirmations, you need to practice using them. First, you need to identify an upcoming goal that you would like to accomplish. Then, you need to write out that goal in simple language. Once you have a clear, concise goal statement written down, you need to transform that statement into an affirmation using the previous three steps. The following is an example of how to turn goal statements into affirmations.

Statement: "In the next few weeks, I will add another product to my internet business."

Affirmation: "In the next few weeks I am adding a terrific new product to my successful internet business."

Notice the differences in the two sentences. By changing the word *will* to the word *am,* and by adding the positive terms *terrific, new* and *successful* the goal statement becomes an affirmation.

If you do not have a specific goal that you are trying to accomplish, you can still use affirmations to improve your positive thinking skills. In this case, you need to choose a positive statement that is general but upbeat in nature. Some examples of these affirmations are…

"I am using my positive thinking skills to succeed in business."

"I am accomplishing great things with positive thoughts and a winning attitude."

"I am an outstanding entrepreneur."

Once you have two or three well-written affirmations completed, you can begin utilizing them on a daily basis. Just as with visualizations, affirmations work best if practiced repeatedly throughout the day. To get the most out of your affirmations it is best to repeat them at least three times a day, usually once upon waking, again in the afternoon and then, once more before bed each night.

By using your new visualization and affirmations skills frequently, you will be better able to set and reach your positive thinking goals.

How to set positive thinking goals

Once you have begun to adopt a positive attitude, it is time to set positive thinking goals. These goals differ from your regular goals in that they concentrate specifically on your quest to learn the art of positive thinking and the benefits that you will enjoy from this quest. These goals should spell out the details of what you wish to accomplish with positive thinking and also contain the specific outcomes of these accomplishments.

There are four steps involved in setting positive thinking goals. By using all four steps, you will create goals that are both attainable and beneficial.

Identify a specific, outcome-oriented goal. This goal will be different from your earlier action-oriented goals in that the goal will concentrate on an eventual positive outcome, not on an immediate task. However, this goal will still need to be specific and detailed. To help determine your goals, ask yourself the following questions.

1. What do I want to accomplish most with my positive thinking?
2. What area of my life could benefit most from the powers of positive thinking?
3. What do I expect to gain from my positive thinking skills?

Once you have an honest answer to each of these questions you can begin to shape your goals. For our purposes, let's assume that the answers to the questions were 1) I want to increase my internet sales, 2) My relationship with my spouse and 3) Better problem solving skills. Each of these answers affords you the basis of a positive thinking goal. For the rest of the steps we will concentrate on defining a goal for the first one.

Now that you have a basic goal idea in mind, you need to state that goal in a specific, outcome-oriented manner. For example, instead of saying, "I want to increase my internet sales" you could say "I am going to use my positive thinking skills to determine my customer's needs in order to increase sales".

Break down the goal into short-term and long-term steps. In order to make the goal more easily attainable, you will need to break it down into a few steps. These steps should contain achievable and realistic outcomes. The first step should include a way to make short-term progress on the goal. For this step you could say, "I am going to include a simple survey on my homepage that will enable me to gather information about my customer's likes and dislikes".

For the second step, you will need to include a long-term outcome prediction for the goal. Your second statement could say, "I am going to use my positive thinking skills to interpret the survey data in a way that allows me to be open to new ideas and suggestions. I am then going to use those new ideas to increase sales."

As you can see in this step, we have taken a lofty goal such as, *increase internet sales*, and with a few simple changes turned it into a positive thinking, outcome-oriented goal.

Set up a way to measure your progress. Now that you have a goal in place, you need to set up a way to measure your progress as you work toward attaining that goal. Without a system of measurement you would be forced to wait until the end to gauge your success. In that instance, you would be unable to use your positive thinking skills to boost your motivation and keep your attitude in check.

The form of measurement that you choose will depend mainly on the type of goal that you have set. In our case, the form of measurement could be an increase in the percentage of sales. In order to accurately gauge your progress, you would first have to gather data about your current sales rate and then determine a suitable increase for your goal.

Let's say that you have decided to aim for an overall increase in sales of 25%. This would mean that by the time you have attained your goal, your internet sales will have increased from their current rate by 25%. As you work toward your goal you can now monitor your success by tracking the increase in percentage increments.

Set a time limit. The next step in your goal setting would include a time limit. Without a time limit in place, your goals can easily turn into distant dreams. In our case, the time limit serves two purposes. One, it gives you another way to track your progress. And two, it gives your plans a deadline.

To help you focus on your goal and keep you motivated to finish, you need to establish a realistic time frame in which to accomplish your goal. For our goal, we might choose a deadline of six months. While this deadline may seem long, it will give you plenty of time to create a survey, gather data information, review the information and then make changes toward your goal. Plus, the deadline allows for a period of time for your new plan to work.

Now that we have an outcome deadline, we need to set progress deadlines. These deadlines are set to help keep you on task and ensure your continued progress. For our goal we may set a deadline of two weeks for creating the survey. Then, set a deadline of one month to gather information form the survey. We would then set a deadline of two weeks to review the survey data and determine what improvements we could make to increase sales. Next, we would set a deadline of one month to implement the changes. Our final deadline would be a period of three months to track the changes in sales, make changes in our process or product as necessary, and then ultimately reach our goal.

As each deadline expires, it is important to review your goal and make sure that your progress is on track. At each review, you may make any changes that are necessary to both your plan and your goal. However, try not to change the time limit, as this can lead to procrastination and eventual defeat.

Involve others. The last step in your positive goal creation is the involvement of others. This step is important to the creation of any positive thinking goal because it utilizes the reinforcement and encouragement that can be obtained from family, friends, and colleagues.

After finishing the first three steps of positive goal setting share your goals and deadlines with those around you. Use them as a sounding board, listen to their advice or thoughts, and let them be connected to your success. By informing others of your goals, you will be able to create a net of strength and support that you can call on if reaching your goal becomes difficult or you get off course.

However, be warned – not just anyone will do. There are negative-thinking people in the world, and connecting them to your network will not lead to a positive outcome. If you have friends or family who are trapped in a cycle of negative thinking, then you need to keep them away from your business. This may seem harsh, but positive thinking doesn't work when there's someone aggressively undermining it with their own negativity.

How finding a mentor can help with positive thinking goals

No matter how much knowledge you possess about your business or how much work you put into realizing your goals; sometimes you need outside advice. While this advice can come from any number of avenues, it is usually most advantageous to seek the guidance of a mentor.

A mentor can be any person with knowledge of your field of business. However, when searching out a mentor, it is best to seek someone who has the greatest understanding of the situation you are facing and the most experience with a business similar to your own. To find a mentor and get the most out of your time together, follow the simple steps below.

Choose a specific situation to seek advice for. While you may wish to seek as much help as possible, it is easier and more beneficial to narrow your quest down to a specific area or situation. Later, after that situation has been resolved, you can also go back to your mentor for additional help.

To choose a situation to pursue, review your positive thinking goals and determine which one is the most important to you or your business. Once you have a goal in mind you will be able to narrow down your choice of mentors by evaluating their level of expertise in your topic. For example, if you choose to seek a mentor to help you increase your internet sales, then you will want to choose someone who has achieved great successes in this area. You do not want to choose someone who hasn't been in business very long, or someone who has vast experience and success in retail sales but not in internet sales.

Choosing a specific situation will also help you later when you go to prepare your list of questions to ask your mentor. By choosing a specific problem and a set of specific questions prior to your first visit, you will give yourself extra time to review the questions and weed out the unnecessary information.

Contact your potential mentor. While this step seems obvious, the way in which you contact the person can be a little tricky. Depending on your level of familiarity with the person, your first contact could consist of something as simple as a quick phone call or something as formal as a written request for an interview. In order to adhere to professional etiquette requirements, your first contact with someone you are not very familiar with should always start with a written request or phone call to his or her secretary. Never call the personal phone number of a person you are not on a comfortable level with.

Also, chances are good that the person you choose as your potential mentor is going to have a busy schedule. Because of this, it is usually best if all contact is begun by setting up an appointment to state your case. Never try to state your case or explain your position during the first contact.

Once you have made an appointment, you need to pick the type of meeting you will have. Depending on the circumstances and the time that your mentor has free, this first meeting can be a short phone call or even a meeting over lunch. If possible, allow your mentor to choose the time and place of the first meeting.

Prepare thoroughly for the meeting. Proper preparation will save both you and your mentor a vast amount of time. With proper preparation you will be able to state your request in a simple, knowledgeable manner. Make sure that you are prepared to share your specific goals and challenges with your mentor and are able to explain to him or her exactly what it is you expect to gain from them.

Ask specific questions. Once someone has agreed to be your mentor, you need to prepare a list of specific question for him or her. If your questions are too broad they will be hard for your mentor to answer. Plus, general questions usually require multiple answers, which can lead to wasted time on both sides.

Using our earlier goal as an example, notice the differences between these sets of questions.

"How can I increase my internet sales?"

"What are three steps I can take to start increasing my internet sales?"

"How can I determine my customer's needs?"

"Have you ever utilized customer surveys? And if so, what is the most important you can tell me about them?"

As you can see from the examples, the second question in each set is more detailed and specific. Recognizing and utilizing this distinction will enable you to prepare better questions and ultimately receive better, more goal-oriented advice.

Put your mentor's advice into action. It is not enough to simply seek the advice of a mentor. You also have to be willing to listen to their ideas, research their ideas and eventually, put them into action. A great idea is just a great idea until it is turned into a goal. Use what you have learned from your mentor to expand upon your goals and increase your chances of success.

Use your mentor for more than just advice. A mentor can be a great source of inspiration and positive thinking. Listen to his or her stories, get caught up in his or her excitement, use his or her positive thinking to bolster your own. If you find your attitude taking a negative turn, or discover thoughts of defeat sneaking into your mental self-talk, call your mentor for a positive pep talk.

Thank your mentor. No matter how the experience ends, whether you ultimately use their advice or not, always send a card or gift of appreciation to your mentor. While this little step may not seem important, it is the biggest and best way to ensure that your professional relationship continues. The fact of the matter is that your mentor probably agreed to help you solely because your success is important to him or her. Let them know that you appreciate their time and effort and keep them abreast of your success. In doing so you will leave an avenue open for further mentoring and new opportunities.

Printed by Libri Plureos GmbH in Hamburg,
Germany